Animal Babies

Chicks

by Kelsey Jopp

FOCUS READERS

SCOUT

www.focusreaders.com

Focus Readers is distributed by North Star Editions:
sales@northstareditions.com | 888-417-0195

Produced for Focus Readers by Red Line Editorial.

Photographs ©: Santirat Praeknokkaew/Shutterstock Images, cover, 1, 11, 16 (top left); Malgorzata Surawska/Shutterstock Images, 4, 16 (top right); CaseyHillPhoto/iStockphoto, 7; Baloncici/Shutterstock Images, 9 (top), 16 (bottom right); MilousSK/Shutterstock Images, 9 (bottom); Vitalii Kirdan/Shutterstock Images, 13; natalie_board/iStockphoto, 15, 16 (bottom left)

Library of Congress Cataloging-in-Publication Data
Names: Jopp, Kelsey, 1993- author.
Title: Chicks / by Kelsey Jopp.
Description: Lake Elmo, MN : Focus Readers, [2020] | Series: Animal babies | Audience: K to Grade 3. | Includes index.
Identifiers: LCCN 2018053615 (print) | LCCN 2018055851 (ebook) | ISBN 9781641859516 (pdf) | ISBN 9781641858823 (e-book) | ISBN 9781641857444 (hardcover) | ISBN 9781641858137 (paperback)
Subjects: LCSH: Chicks--Juvenile literature.
Classification: LCC SF498.4 (ebook) | LCC SF498.4 .J67 2020 (print) | DDC 636.5--dc23
LC record available at https://lccn.loc.gov/2018053615

Printed in the United States of America
Mankato, MN
May, 2019

About the Author

Kelsey Jopp is an editor, writer, and lifelong learner. She lives in Saint Paul, Minnesota, where she enjoys doing yoga and playing endless fetch with her sheltie, Teddy.

Table of Contents

egg
feathers

First Days

Chicks are baby chickens.

They hatch from eggs.

They are small.

They have **feathers**.

Chicks open their eyes.
Chicks move around.
Chicks keep one
another warm.

eye

Changes

Chicks get older.

They eat **feed**.

They drink water.

They sleep a lot.

feed

Chicks grow fast.

Their legs get longer.

Their **beaks** get bigger.

beak
legs

Chicks grow new feathers.

The feathers are long.

Growing Up

Chicks keep growing.

They move to a **coop**.

They become adults.

coop

Glossary

beaks

feathers

coop

feed

Index